Super Scrumptious Scone Cookbook

Delicious Scone Recipes for All Occasions

BY: Nancy Silverman

COPYRIGHT NOTICES

Table of Contents

Introduction

Scones are a classic breakfast food that everyone loves. They are more flavorful and filling than a muffin and easier to eat on-the-go than a plate of breakfast eggs. In addition, scones can be made in so many different ways! Our cookbook will help you make tons of different scones that all taste as if they just came out of a bakery. You'll never need to pay for that coffee shop scone again- you can easily make incredible scones with just one big bowl, a baking tray and an oven!

I have always loved scones and wanted to bring some of my favorite scone recipes to you. I wanted to share the awesome flavor combinations I have discovered that make morning scones something to really look forward to. Mostly, I wanted to write a cookbook that showed how easy making scones could be! All of my recipes take about 15 minutes to put together and another 15 minutes to bake to golden perfection. That means you can be eating delicious, fresh scones in under 30 minutes! The recipes are easy to follow and require very few steps. It is astounding how easy scones can be!

While I recommend starting off with a simple recipe like the cinnamon scones or the healthy whole wheat scones. Then, branch out and give the pumpkin chocolate chip scones a try or, if you are craving a savory scone, the ham and cheddar scones are a clear winner. Once you have mastered those recipes, give the interesting rosemary scones a try or maybe the scones made with brie- I guarantee you have never tried anything like those before!

Get out a big mixing bowl and your measuring cups, preheat your oven and get ready to make some awesome scones. While the recipes all make at least 10 scones, we know you will want to eat more than one- they are irresistible when they are hot out of the oven! Enjoy!

Cinnamon Scones

This simple scone recipe is wonderful for any time of year. It has a delicious cinnamon taste and doesn't require many ingredients at all to put together. Everyone can make these great scones!

Active Time: 15 minutes

Cook Time: 15 minutes

Yield: 10 servings

Ingredients:

- ¼ cup brown sugar
- 2 ¼ cups flour
- 1/8 tsp kosher salt
- 1 ½ tsp ground cinnamon
- 1 Tbsp baking powder
- 8 Tbsp butter, room temperature
- 2 large eggs
- ½ cup heavy cream
- ¾ tsp vanilla extract
- 2 Tbsp white granulated sugar
- 2 Tbsp milk

Directions:

1. First, preheat an oven to 350 degrees F and prepared a sheet tray by lining it with a piece of parchment paper.

2. Second, in a large bowl, combine the flour, cinnamon, brown sugar, salt and baking powder. Stir to mix together well.

3. Add the butter, then blend it into the dry mix using your hands until it resembled coarse crumbles.

4. Add the eggs, heavy cream and vanilla extract and mix the ingredients together to form a thick dough.

5. Next, turn the dough out onto your floured surface. Then, roll into a ball.

6. Flatten the ball into a 1" thick round disc.

7. Cut the disc into 10 triangles then place then on the prepared sheet tray.

8. Brush the scones with the milk then sprinkle with the white granulated sugar.

9. Bake in the preheated oven for 15 minutes or until the edges are golden brown.

10. Remove the tray from the oven. Then, move the scones to a cooling rack.

11. Enjoy warm!

Sour Cream Scones

Sour cream scones are a classic that belongs on any tea table. They are a wonderful, simple scone that is made irresistible by the slight tang of sour cream which pairs perfectly with the sweet scone.

Active Time: 15 minutes

Cook Time: 15 minutes

Yield: 10 servings

Ingredients:

- 2 ¼ cups flour
- 1/8 tsp kosher salt
- 1 Tbsp baking powder
- ¼ cup brown sugar
- ¼ tsp lemon zest
- 8 Tbsp butter, room temperature
- 2 large eggs
- ½ cup sour cream
- ¾ tsp vanilla extract
- 2 Tbsp white granulated sugar
- 2 Tbsp milk

Directions:

1. First, preheat an oven to 350 degrees F and prepared a sheet tray by lining it with a piece of parchment paper.

2. Second, in a large bowl, combine the flour, lemon zest, brown sugar, salt and baking powder. Stir to mix together well.

3. Add the butter, then blend it into the dry mix using your hands until it resembled coarse crumbles.

4. Add the vanilla extract, sour cream and eggs. Then, mix the ingredients together to form a thick dough.

5. Next, turn the dough out onto your floured surface. Then, roll into a ball.

6. Flatten the ball into a 1" thick round disc.

7. Cut the disc into 10 triangles then place then on the prepared sheet tray.

8. Brush the scones with the milk then sprinkle with the white granulated sugar.

9. Bake in the preheated oven for 15 minutes or until the edges are golden brown.

10. Remove the tray from the oven. Then, move the scones to a cooling rack.

11. Enjoy warm!

Blueberry Scones

Blueberry scones are a summertime favorite. Find a nearby place to pick some blueberries and then use them to make this great breakfast recipe. Your morning will be great with an amazing, homemade scone!

Active Time: 15 minutes

Cook Time: 15 minutes

Yield: 10 servings

Ingredients:

- ¼ cup brown sugar
- 2 ¼ cups flour
- 1/8 tsp kosher salt
- ¼ tsp lemon zest
- 1 Tbsp baking powder
- 8 Tbsp butter, room temperature
- 2 large eggs
- ½ cup sour cream
- ¾ tsp vanilla extract
- 1 cup fresh blueberries
- 2 Tbsp white granulated sugar
- 2 Tbsp milk

Directions:

1. First, preheat an oven to 350 degrees F and prepared a sheet tray by lining it with a piece of parchment paper.

2. Second, in a large bowl, combine the flour, salt, lemon zest, brown sugar and baking powder. Stir to mix together well.

3. Add the butter, then blend it into the dry mix using your hands until it resembled coarse crumbles.

4. Add the vanilla extract, sour cream and eggs and mix the ingredients together to form a thick dough.

5. Gently fold the blueberries into the dough. Try not to smash them too much but if a few get crushed, that is okay!

6. Next, turn the dough out onto your floured surface. Then, roll into a ball.

7. Flatten the ball into a 1" thick round disc.

8. Cut the disc into 10 triangles then place then on the prepared sheet tray.

9. Brush the scones with the milk then sprinkle with the white granulated sugar.

10. Bake in the preheated oven for 15 minutes or until the edges are golden brown.

11. Remove the tray from the oven. Then, move the scones to a cooling rack.

12. Enjoy warm!

Raspberry Scones

Raspberry scones are a classic scone that everyone will love. While this recipe uses raspberry jam to make a beautiful swirl throughout the scones, feel free to add up to ½ cup fresh raspberries as well for even more flavor!

Active Time: 20 minutes

Cook Time: 15 minutes

Yield: 10 servings

Ingredients:

- ¼ cup brown sugar
- 2 ½ cups flour
- 1/8 tsp kosher salt
- ¼ tsp lemon zest
- 1 Tbsp baking powder
- 8 Tbsp butter, room temperature
- 2 large eggs
- ½ cup sour cream
- ¾ tsp vanilla extract
- ½ cup raspberry jam
- 2 Tbsp white granulated sugar
- 2 Tbsp milk

Directions:

1. First, preheat an oven to 350 degrees F and prepared a sheet tray by lining it with a piece of parchment paper.

2. Second, in a large bowl, combine the flour, salt, lemon zest, brown sugar and baking powder. Stir to mix together well.

3. Add the butter, then blend it into the dry mix using your hands until it resembled coarse crumbles.

4. Add the eggs, sour cream and vanilla extract and mix the ingredients together to form a thick dough.

5. Next, turn the dough out onto your floured surface. Then, roll into a ball.

6. Flatten the ball into a 1" thick round disc.

7. Spread the jam across the disc and then fold in in half and in half again. Roll the dough back into a ball and flatten it once more into a 1" thick disc- the jam should be nicely swirled in.

8. Cut the disc into 10 triangles then place then on the prepared sheet tray.

9. Brush the scones with the milk then sprinkle with the white granulated sugar.

10. Bake in the preheated oven for 15 minutes or until the edges are golden brown.

11. Remove the tray from the oven. Then, move the scones to a cooling rack.

12. Enjoy warm!

Raspberry White Chocolate Scones

You can find raspberry white chocolate scones on many café menus but why go all the way to a café to buy one when you can make them at home! This recipe is café worthy but without the extra trip.

Active Time: 20 minutes

Cook Time: 15 minutes

Yield: 12 servings

Ingredients:

- 2 ½ cups flour
- 1/8 tsp kosher salt
- ¼ cup brown sugar
- ¼ tsp lemon zest
- 1 Tbsp baking powder
- 8 Tbsp butter, room temperature
- 2 large eggs
- ½ cup sour cream
- ¾ tsp vanilla extract
- ½ cup white chocolate chips
- ½ cup raspberry jam
- 2 Tbsp white granulated sugar
- 2 Tbsp milk

Directions:

1. First, preheat an oven to 350 degrees F and prepared a sheet tray by lining it with a piece of parchment paper.

2. Second, in a large bowl, combine the flour, salt, lemon zest, brown sugar and baking powder. Stir to mix together well.

3. Add the butter, then blend it into the dry mix using your hands until it resembled coarse crumbles.

4. Add the vanilla extract, sour cream and eggs and mix the ingredients together to form a thick dough.

5. Add the white chocolate chips and fold them gently into the dough.

6. Next, turn the dough out onto your floured surface. Then, roll into a ball.

7. Flatten the ball into a 1" thick round disc.

8. Spread the jam across the disc and then fold in in half and in half again. Roll the dough back into a ball. Then, flatten it once more into a 1" thick disc- the jam should be nicely swirled in.

9. Cut the disc into 12 triangles then place then on the prepared sheet tray.

10. Brush the scones with the milk then sprinkle with the white granulated sugar.

11. Bake in the preheated oven for 15 minutes or until the edges are golden brown.

12. Remove the tray from the oven. Then, move the scones to a cooling rack. Enjoy warm!

Blackberry Scones

Blackberry scones are a unique treat that is sure to please your guests. Make a double batch and freeze some of the dough to bake later when you crave these scones again.

Active Time: 20 minutes

Cook Time: 15 minutes

Yield: 10 servings

Ingredients:

- ¼ cup brown sugar
- 2 ½ cups flour
- 1/8 tsp kosher salt
- ¼ tsp lemon zest
- 1 Tbsp baking powder
- 8 Tbsp butter, room temperature
- 2 large eggs
- ½ cup sour cream
- ¾ tsp vanilla extract
- ½ cup blackberry jam
- 2 Tbsp white granulated sugar
- 2 Tbsp milk

Directions:

1. First, preheat an oven to 350 degrees F and prepared a sheet tray by lining it with a piece of parchment paper.

2. Second, in a large bowl, combine the flour, salt, lemon zest, brown sugar and baking powder. Stir to mix together well.

3. Add the butter, then blend it into the dry mix using your hands until it resembled coarse crumbles.

4. Add the vanilla extract, sour cream and eggs and mix the ingredients together to form a thick dough.

5. Next, turn the dough out onto your floured surface. Then, roll into a ball.

6. Flatten the ball into a 1" thick round disc.

7. Spread the jam across the disc and then fold in in half and in half again. Roll the dough back into a ball. Then, flatten it once more into a 1" thick disc- the jam should be nicely swirled in.

8. Cut the disc into 10 triangles then place then on the prepared sheet tray.

9. Brush the scones with the milk then sprinkle with the white granulated sugar.

10. Bake in the preheated oven for 15 minutes or until the edges are golden brown.

11. Remove the tray from the oven. Then, move the scones to a cooling rack.

12. Enjoy warm!

Spiced Scones

This is a wonderful scone recipe to make in the winter when warm spices are appreciated. We have found the perfect blend of spices to make these scones flavorful yet simple enough to make in just a few minutes.

Active Time: 15 minutes

Cook Time: 15 minutes

Yield: 10 servings

Ingredients:

- 2 ¼ cups flour
- 1/8 tsp kosher salt
- ¼ tsp ground nutmeg
- ¼ tsp ground ginger
- 3/4 tsp ground cinnamon
- 1/8 tsp ground cloves
- 1 Tbsp baking powder
- ¼ cup brown sugar
- 8 Tbsp butter, room temperature
- 2 large eggs
- ½ cup heavy cream
- ¾ tsp vanilla extract
- 2 Tbsp white granulated sugar
- 2 Tbsp milk

Directions:

1. First, preheat an oven to 350 degrees F and prepared a sheet tray by lining it with a piece of parchment paper.

2. Second, in a large bowl, combine the flour, salt, nutmeg, cinnamon, ginger, cloves, brown sugar and baking powder. Stir to mix together well.

3. Add the butter, then blend it into the dry mix using your hands until it resembled coarse crumbles.

4. Add the eggs, heavy cream and vanilla extract and mix the ingredients together to form a thick dough.

5. Next, turn the dough out onto your floured surface. Then, roll into a ball.

6. Flatten the ball into a 1" thick round disc.

7. Cut the disc into 10 triangles then place then on the prepared sheet tray.

8. Brush the scones with the milk then sprinkle with the white granulated sugar.

9. Bake in the preheated oven for 15 minutes or until the edges are golden brown.

10. Remove the tray from the oven. Then, move the scones to a cooling rack.

11. Enjoy warm!

Chocolate Chip Scones

Everyone needs a good chocolate chips scone recipe, and ours can't be beaten! Cream based scones are the best match for chocolate chips, and we know that this recipe will definitely be an instant hit in your home.

Active Time: 15 minutes

Cook Time: 15 minutes

Yield: 12 servings

Ingredients:

- ¼ cup brown sugar
- 2 ¼ cups flour
- 1/8 tsp kosher salt
- 1 ½ tsp ground cinnamon
- 1 Tbsp baking powder
- 8 Tbsp butter, room temperature
- 2 large eggs
- ½ cup heavy cream
- 1 cup mini chocolate chips
- ¾ tsp vanilla extract
- 2 Tbsp white granulated sugar
- 2 Tbsp milk

Directions:

1. First, preheat an oven to 350 degrees F and prepared a sheet tray by lining it with a piece of parchment paper.

2. Second, in a large bowl, combine the flour, cinnamon, salt, brown sugar and baking powder. Stir to mix together well.

3. Add the butter, then blend it into the dry mix using your hands until it resembled coarse crumbles.

4. Add the eggs, heavy cream and vanilla extract and mix the ingredients together to form a thick dough.

5. Fold the mini chocolate chips into your dough.

6. Next, turn the dough out onto your floured surface. Then, roll into a ball.

7. Flatten the ball into a 1" thick round disc.

8. Cut the disc into 12 triangles then place then on the prepared sheet tray.

9. Brush the scones with the milk then sprinkle with the white granulated sugar.

10. Bake in the preheated oven for 15 minutes or until the edges are golden brown.

11. Remove the tray from the oven. Then, move the scones to a cooling rack.

12. Enjoy warm!

White Chocolate Chip Scones

Sweet white chocolate is a great addition to a scone and will give you a little extra sugar to get you going in the morning. While these are a classic breakfast food, they are tasty enough to enjoy as dessert too!

Active Time: 15 minutes

Cook Time: 15 minutes

Yield: 12 servings

Ingredients:

- ¼ cup brown sugar
- 2 ¼ cups flour
- 1/8 tsp kosher salt
- 1 ½ tsp ground cinnamon
- 1 Tbsp baking powder
- 8 Tbsp butter, room temperature
- 2 large eggs
- ½ cup heavy cream
- ¾ tsp vanilla extract
- 1 cup white chocolate chips
- 2 Tbsp white granulated sugar
- 2 Tbsp milk

Directions:

1. First, preheat an oven to 350 degrees F and prepared a sheet tray by lining it with a piece of parchment paper.

2. Second, in a large bowl, combine the flour, cinnamon, salt, brown sugar and baking powder. Stir to mix together well.

3. Add the butter, then blend it into the dry mix using your hands until it resembled coarse crumbles.

4. Add the eggs, heavy cream and vanilla extract and mix the ingredients together to form a thick dough.

5. Fold the white chocolate chips into your dough.

6. Next, turn the dough out onto your floured surface. Then, roll into a ball.

7. Flatten the ball into a 1" thick round disc.

8. Cut the disc into 12 triangles then place then on the prepared sheet tray.

9. Brush the scones with the milk then sprinkle with the white granulated sugar.

10. Bake in the preheated oven for 15 minutes or until the edges are golden brown.

11. Remove the tray from the oven. Then, move the scones to a cooling rack.

12. Enjoy warm!

Cinnamon Chip Scones

When the weather starts to cool and fall flavors are abundant, these scones make for a wonderful breakfast option. If you can't find cinnamon chips in a grocery store nearby, you can definitely order them online to be delivered right to your door!

Active Time: 15 minutes

Cook Time: 15 minutes

Yield: 12 servings

Ingredients:

- 2 ¼ cups flour
- 1 Tbsp baking powder
- 1/8 tsp kosher salt
- 1 ½ tsp ground cinnamon
- ¼ cup brown sugar
- 8 Tbsp butter, room temperature
- 2 large eggs
- ½ cup heavy cream
- 1 cup cinnamon chocolate chips
- ¾ tsp vanilla extract
- 2 Tbsp white granulated sugar
- 2 Tbsp milk

Directions:

1. First, preheat an oven to 350 degrees F and prepared a sheet tray by lining it with a piece of parchment paper.

2. Second, in a large bowl, combine the flour, cinnamon, salt, brown sugar and baking powder. Stir to mix together well.

3. Add the butter, then blend it into the dry mix using your hands until it resembled coarse crumbles.

4. Add the eggs, heavy cream and vanilla extract and mix the ingredients together to form a thick dough.

5. Fold the cinnamon chips into the dough.

6. Next, turn the dough out onto your floured surface. Then, roll into a ball.

7. Flatten the ball into a 1" thick round disc.

8. Cut the disc into 12 triangles then place then on the prepared sheet tray.

9. Brush the scones with the milk then sprinkle with the white granulated sugar.

10. Bake in the preheated oven for 15 minutes or until the edges are golden brown.

11. Remove the tray from the oven. Then, move the scones to a cooling rack.

12. Enjoy warm!

Mixed Berry Scones

Every bite of these scones is bursting with berry taste that you won't be able to resist. Use frozen berries to ensure they don't get smashed as you mix the dough.

Active Time: 15 minutes

Cook Time: 15 minutes

Yield: 12 servings

Ingredients:

- ¼ cup brown sugar
- 2 ¼ cups flour
- ¼ tsp ground cinnamon
- 1/8 tsp kosher salt
- 1 Tbsp baking powder
- 8 Tbsp butter, room temperature
- 2 large eggs
- ½ cup heavy cream
- ¾ tsp vanilla extract
- 1 cup frozen mixed berries
- 2 Tbsp white granulated sugar
- 2 Tbsp milk

Directions:

1. First, preheat an oven to 350 degrees F and prepared a sheet tray by lining it with a piece of parchment paper.

2. Second, in a large bowl, combine the flour, cinnamon, salt, brown sugar and baking powder. Stir to mix together well.

3. Add the butter, then blend it into the dry mix using your hands until it resembled coarse crumbles.

4. Add the eggs, heavy cream and vanilla extract and mix the ingredients together to form a thick dough.

5. Fold the frozen berries into the dough.

6. Next, turn the dough out onto your floured surface. Then, roll into a ball.

7. Flatten the ball into a 1" thick round disc.

8. Cut the disc into 12 triangles then place then on the prepared sheet tray.

9. Brush the scones with the milk then sprinkle with the white granulated sugar.

10. Bake in the preheated oven for 15 minutes or until the edges are golden brown.

11. Remove the tray from the oven. Then, move the scones to a cooling rack.

12. Enjoy warm!

Whole Wheat Scones

These scones are made with whole wheat flour which gives them some great extra nutrition that you are sure to love. Use this recipe as a base, and do add in any dried fruit or nuts that you love to make it your own!

Active Time: 15 minutes

Cook Time: 15 minutes

Yield: 10 servings

Ingredients:

- 2 cups whole wheat flour
- 1/8 tsp kosher salt
- ½ tsp ground nutmeg
- 1 tsp ground cinnamon
- 1 Tbsp baking powder
- ¼ cup brown sugar
- 8 Tbsp butter, room temperature
- 2 large eggs
- ½ cup heavy cream
- ¾ tsp vanilla extract
- 2 Tbsp brown granulated sugar
- 2 Tbsp milk

Directions:

1. First, preheat an oven to 350 degrees F and prepared a sheet tray by lining it with a piece of parchment paper.

2. Second, in a large bowl, combine the flour, salt, cinnamon, nutmeg, ¼ cup brown sugar and baking powder. Stir to mix together well.

3. Add the butter, then blend it into the dry mix using your hands until it resembled coarse crumbles.

4. Add the eggs, heavy cream and vanilla extract and mix the ingredients together to form a thick dough.

5. Next, turn the dough out onto your floured surface. Then, roll into a ball.

6. Flatten the ball into a 1" thick round disc.

7. Cut the disc into 10 triangles then place then on the prepared sheet tray.

8. Brush the scones with the milk then sprinkle with the remaining brown sugar.

9. Bake in the preheated oven for 15 minutes or until the edges are golden brown.

10. Remove the tray from the oven. Then, move the scones to a cooling rack.

11. Enjoy warm!

Almond Scones

Everyone loves a good almond scone to start the day! This recipe is quick to make and bursting with almond flavor so it will be a clear breakfast winner.

Active Time: 15 minutes

Cook Time: 15 minutes

Yield: 10 servings

Ingredients:

- ¼ cup brown sugar
- 2 ¼ cups flour
- 1/8 tsp kosher salt
- 1 ½ tsp ground cinnamon
- 1 Tbsp baking powder
- 8 Tbsp butter, room temperature
- 2 large eggs
- ½ cup heavy cream
- 1 tsp almond extract
- 1 cup sliced almonds
- 2 Tbsp white granulated sugar
- 2 Tbsp milk

Directions:

1. First, preheat an oven to 350 degrees F and prepared a sheet tray by lining it with a piece of parchment paper.

2. Second, in a large bowl, combine the flour, cinnamon, salt, brown sugar and baking powder. Stir to mix together well.

3. Add the butter, then blend it into the dry mix using your hands until it resembled coarse crumbles.

4. Add the eggs, heavy cream and almond extract and mix the ingredients together to form a thick dough.

5. Fold in the sliced almonds- it is okay if they break as you mix them in as it will just make nice small pieces throughout your scones!

6. Next, turn the dough out onto your floured surface. Then, roll into a ball.

7. Flatten the ball into a 1" thick round disc.

8. Cut the disc into 10 triangles then place then on the prepared sheet tray.

9. Brush the scones with the milk then sprinkle with the white granulated sugar.

10. Bake in the preheated oven for 15 minutes or until the edges are golden brown.

11. Remove the tray from the oven. Then, move the scones to a cooling rack.

12. Enjoy warm!

Apricot Scones

Dried fruit is a fantastic addition to any kind of scone, and these apricot scones are no exception. Use your sharp pair of kitchen shears to quickly cut whole, dried apricots into smaller pieces.

Active Time: 15 minutes

Cook Time: 15 minutes

Yield: 12 servings

Ingredients:

- ¼ cup brown sugar
- 2 ¼ cups flour
- 1/8 tsp kosher salt
- ½ tsp ground cinnamon
- 1 Tbsp baking powder
- 8 Tbsp butter, room temperature
- 1 tsp lemon zest
- 2 large eggs
- ½ cup heavy cream
- ¾ tsp vanilla extract
- 1 cup chopped dried apricots
- 2 Tbsp white granulated sugar
- 2 Tbsp milk

Directions:

1. First, preheat an oven to 350 degrees F and prepared a sheet tray by lining it with a piece of parchment paper.

2. Second, in a large bowl, combine the flour, salt, cinnamon, brown sugar, lemon zest and baking powder. Stir to mix together well.

3. Add the butter, then blend it into the dry mix using your hands until it resembled coarse crumbles.

4. Add the eggs, heavy cream and vanilla extract and mix the ingredients together to form a thick dough.

5. Stir in the chopped almonds and mix into the dough to evenly distribute.

6. Next, turn the dough out onto your floured surface. Then, roll into a ball.

7. Flatten the ball into a 1" thick round disc.

8. Cut the disc into 12 triangles then place then on the prepared sheet tray.

9. Brush the scones with the milk then sprinkle with the white granulated sugar.

10. Bake in the preheated oven for 15 minutes or until the edges are golden brown.

11. Remove the tray from the oven. Then, move the scones to a cooling rack.

12. Enjoy warm!

Cranberry Orange Scones

While cranberry and orange are a bright and summery flavor, these scones are actually perfect for the wintertime when citrus is in season. The bright red cranberries are also quite festive and perfect for the holidays!

Active Time: 15 minutes

Cook Time: 15 minutes

Yield: 10 servings

Ingredients:

- ¼ cup brown sugar
- 2 ¼ cups flour
- 1/8 tsp kosher salt
- 1 tsp orange zest
- 1 Tbsp baking powder
- 8 Tbsp butter, room temperature
- 2 large eggs
- ¼ cup heavy cream
- ¼ cup orange juice
- ¾ tsp vanilla extract
- 1 cup dried cranberries
- 2 Tbsp white granulated sugar
- 2 Tbsp milk

Directions:

1. First, preheat an oven to 350 degrees F and prepared a sheet tray by lining it with a piece of parchment paper.

2. Second, in a large bowl, combine the flour, salt, orange zest, brown sugar and baking powder. Stir to mix together well.

3. Add the butter, then blend it into the dry mix using your hands until it resembled coarse crumbles.

4. Add the eggs, heavy cream, orange juice and vanilla extract and mix the ingredients together to form a thick dough.

5. Stir in the dried cranberries, mixing until they are evenly distributed throughout the dough.

6. Next, turn the dough out onto your floured surface. Then, roll into a ball.

7. Flatten the ball into a 1" thick round disc.

8. Cut the disc into 10 triangles then place then on the prepared sheet tray.

9. Brush the scones with the milk then sprinkle with the white granulated sugar.

10. Bake in the preheated oven for 15 minutes or until the edges are golden brown.

11. Remove the tray from the oven. Then, move the scones to a cooling rack.

12. Enjoy warm!

Gingerbread Scones

We love these scones around Christmastime when gingerbread is all around. The powerful taste is perfect for a cold winters morning and will definitely make your morning festive.

Active Time: 15 minutes

Cook Time: 15 minutes

Yield: 10 servings

Ingredients:

- 2 ¼ cups flour
- 1/8 tsp kosher salt
- ¼ tsp ground nutmeg
- 1 tsp ground cinnamon
- 1 tsp ground ginger
- 1 Tbsp baking powder
- ¼ cup dark molasses
- 8 Tbsp butter, room temperature
- 2 large eggs
- ½ cup heavy cream
- ¾ tsp vanilla extract
- 2 Tbsp brown sugar
- 2 Tbsp milk

Directions:

1. First, preheat an oven to 350 degrees F and prepared a sheet tray by lining it with a piece of parchment paper.

2. Second, in a large bowl, combine the flour, salt, cinnamon, ginger, nutmeg and baking powder. Stir to mix together well.

3. Add the butter, then blend it into the dry mix using your hands until it resembled coarse crumbles.

4. Add the eggs, heavy cream, molasses and vanilla extract and mix the ingredients together to form a thick dough.

5. Next, turn the dough out onto your floured surface. Then, roll into a ball.

6. Flatten the ball into a 1" thick round disc.

7. Cut the disc into 10 triangles then place then on the prepared sheet tray.

8. Brush the scones with the milk then sprinkle with the brown sugar.

9. Bake in the preheated oven for 15 minutes or until the edges are golden brown.

10. Remove the tray from the oven. Then, move the scones to a cooling rack.

11. Enjoy warm!

Nutella Scones

If you do love sweet treats in the morning, this recipe is perfect for you! Nutella is swirled into the scone dough to make a wonderful, irresistible breakfast we know you will love.

Active Time: 20 minutes

Cook Time: 15 minutes

Yield: 10 servings

Ingredients:

- ¼ cup brown sugar
- 2 ¼ cups flour
- 1/8 tsp kosher salt
- ½ tsp ground cinnamon
- 1 Tbsp baking powder
- 8 Tbsp butter, room temperature
- 2 large eggs
- ½ cup heavy cream
- ¾ tsp vanilla extract
- ½ cup nutella
- 2 Tbsp white granulated sugar
- 2 Tbsp milk

Directions:

1. First, preheat an oven to 350 degrees F and prepared a sheet tray by lining it with a piece of parchment paper.

2. Second, in a large bowl, combine the flour, cinnamon, salt, brown sugar and baking powder. Stir to mix together well.

3. Add the butter, then blend it into the dry mix using your hands until it resembled coarse crumbles.

4. Add the eggs, heavy cream and vanilla extract and mix the ingredients together to form a thick dough.

5. Next, turn the dough out onto your floured surface. Then, roll into a ball.

6. Flatten the ball into a 1" thick round disc.

7. Spread the nutella across the dough and fold it in half and in half again. Roll the dough back into a ball. Then, flatten it again into a one inch thick disc. The nutella should be nicely swirled into the dough.

8. Cut the disc into 10 triangles then place then on the prepared sheet tray.

9. Brush the scones with the milk then sprinkle with the white granulated sugar.

10. Bake in the preheated oven for 15 minutes or until the edges are golden brown.

11. Remove the tray from the oven. Then, move the scones to a cooling rack.

12. Enjoy warm!

Ham and Cheese Scones

Savory scones are one of our favorite ways to enjoy a scone and also eat a complete meal. These are perfect for weekday breakfast when you need to eat in a rush- make big batch on the weekend. You will have a perfect to-go breakfast for the whole week!

Active Time: 15 minutes

Cook Time: 15 minutes

Yield: 12 servings

Ingredients:

- ¼ cup brown sugar
- 2 ¼ cups flour
- 1/8 tsp kosher salt
- 1 ½ tsp ground cinnamon
- 1 Tbsp baking powder
- 8 Tbsp butter, room temperature
- 1 cup chopped, cooked ham
- 1 cup shredded cheddar cheese
- 2 large eggs
- ½ cup heavy cream
- ¾ tsp vanilla extract
- 2 Tbsp white granulated sugar
- 2 Tbsp milk

Directions:

1. First, preheat an oven to 350 degrees F and prepared a sheet tray by lining it with a piece of parchment paper.

2. Second, in a large bowl, combine the flour, cinnamon, salt, brown sugar and baking powder. Stir to mix together well.

3. Add the butter, then blend it into the dry mix using your hands until it resembled coarse crumbles.

4. Stir the ham and cheese into the mix.

5. Add the eggs, heavy cream and vanilla extract and mix the ingredients together to form a thick dough.

6. Next, turn the dough out onto your floured surface. Then, roll into a ball.

7. Flatten the ball into a 1" thick round disc.

8. Cut the disc into 12 triangles then place then on the prepared sheet tray.

9. Brush the scones with the milk then sprinkle with the white granulated sugar.

10. Bake in the preheated oven for 15 minutes or until the edges are golden brown.

11. Remove the tray from the oven. Then, move the scones to a cooling rack.

12. Enjoy warm!

Lemon Poppy Seed Scones

The beautiful poppy seeds that's are mixed into these scones will look wonderful on your next brunch table. The bright lemon flavor will also make each bite a delicious treat.

Active Time: 15 minutes

Cook Time: 15 minutes

Yield: 10 servings

Ingredients:

- ¼ cup brown sugar
- 2 ¼ cups flour
- 1/8 tsp kosher salt
- 1 tsp lemon zest
- 1 Tbsp baking powder
- 8 Tbsp butter, room temperature
- 2 large eggs
- ½ cup heavy cream
- ½ tsp lemon extract
- ¼ cup poppy seeds
- 2 Tbsp white granulated sugar
- 2 Tbsp milk

Directions:

1. First, preheat an oven to 350 degrees F and prepared a sheet tray by lining it with a piece of parchment paper.

2. Second, in a large bowl, combine the flour, salt, lemon zest, poppy seeds, brown sugar and baking powder. Stir to mix together well.

3. Add the butter, then blend it into the dry mix using your hands until it resembled coarse crumbles.

4. Add the eggs, heavy cream and lemon extract and mix the ingredients together to form a thick dough.

5. Next, turn the dough out onto your floured surface. Then, roll into a ball.

6. Flatten the ball into a 1" thick round disc.

7. Cut the disc into 10 triangles then place then on the prepared sheet tray.

8. Brush the scones with the milk then sprinkle with the white granulated sugar.

9. Bake in the preheated oven for 15 minutes or until the edges are golden brown.

10. Remove the tray from the oven. Then, move the scones to a cooling rack.

11. Enjoy warm!

Oatmeal Scones

When you can't definitely decide if you want a big bowl of oatmeal or a scone for breakfast, why not have both! These scones are made with rolled oats which not only add a hearty taste but also some great nutrition to each scone.

Active Time: 15 minutes

Cook Time: 15 minutes

Yield: 10 servings

Ingredients:

- 1 ¼ cups flour
- 1 cup rolled oats
- 1/8 tsp kosher salt
- 1 tsp ground cinnamon
- 1 tsp lemon zest
- 1 Tbsp baking powder
- ¼ cup brown sugar
- 8 Tbsp butter, room temperature
- 2 large eggs
- ½ cup heavy cream
- ¾ tsp vanilla extract
- ½ cup dried blueberries
- 2 Tbsp white granulated sugar
- 2 Tbsp milk

Directions:

1. First, preheat an oven to 350 degrees F and prepared a sheet tray by lining it with a piece of parchment paper.

2. Second, in a large bowl, combine the flour, rolled oats, salt, cinnamon, lemon zest, brown sugar and baking powder. Stir to mix together well.

3. Add the butter, then blend it into the dry mix using your hands until it resembled coarse crumbles.

4. Add the eggs, heavy cream and vanilla extract and mix the ingredients together to form a thick dough.

5. Fold in the dried blueberries, mixing until they are evenly distributed throughout the dough.

6. Next, turn the dough out onto your floured surface. Then, roll into a ball.

7. Flatten the ball into a 1" thick round disc.

8. Cut the disc into 10 triangles then place then on the prepared sheet tray.

9. Brush the scones with the milk then sprinkle with the white granulated sugar.

10. Bake in the preheated oven for 15 minutes or until the edges are golden brown.

11. Remove the tray from the oven. Then, move the scones to a cooling rack. Enjoy warm!

Pumpkin Spice Scones

A warm scone bursting with pumpkin spice flavor is something you will crave after just one bite of these delicious scones. While this recipe is great for the fall when pumpkins are in season, it is worthy of eating any time of year!

Active Time: 15 minutes

Cook Time: 15 minutes

Yield: 10 servings

Ingredients:

- ½ cup pumpkin puree
- 2 ¼ cups flour
- ½ cup heavy cream
- ¼ cup brown sugar
- 1/8 tsp kosher salt
- 1 ½ tsp pumpkin spice
- 1 Tbsp baking powder
- 6 Tbsp butter, room temperature
- 1 large egg
- ¾ tsp vanilla extract
- 2 Tbsp white granulated sugar
- 2 Tbsp milk

Directions:

1. First, preheat an oven to 350 degrees F and prepared a sheet tray by lining it with a piece of parchment paper.

2. Second, in a large bowl, combine the flour, salt, pumpkin spice, brown sugar and baking powder. Stir to mix together well.

3. Add the butter, then blend it into the dry mix using your hands until it resembled coarse crumbles.

4. Add the egg, pumpkin puree, heavy cream and vanilla extract and mix the ingredients together to form a thick dough.

5. Next, turn the dough out onto your floured surface. Then, roll into a ball.

6. Flatten the ball into a 1" thick round disc.

7. Cut the disc into 10 triangles then place then on the prepared sheet tray.

8. Brush the scones with the milk then sprinkle with the white granulated sugar.

9. Bake in the preheated oven for 15 minutes or until the edges are golden brown.

10. Remove the tray from the oven. Then, move the scones to a cooling rack.

11. Enjoy warm!

Apple Cheddar Scones

Apple and cheddar are a great combination that will give your scones a little bit of sweetness and also some great salty taste. This recipe is great for breakfast but is also wonderful for lunch!

Active Time: 15 minutes

Cook Time: 15 minutes

Yield: 14 servings

Ingredients:

- ¼ cup brown sugar
- 2 ¼ cups flour
- 1/8 tsp kosher salt
- ¼ tsp ground cinnamon
- 1 Tbsp baking powder
- 1 cup shredded cheddar cheese
- 8 Tbsp butter, room temperature
- 2 large eggs
- ½ cup heavy cream
- ¾ tsp vanilla extract
- 1 cup chopped apple
- 2 Tbsp white granulated sugar
- 2 Tbsp milk

Directions:

1. First, preheat an oven to 350 degrees F and prepared a sheet tray by lining it with a piece of parchment paper.

2. Second, in a large bowl, combine the flour, salt, cinnamon, brown sugar, cheddar cheese and baking powder. Stir to mix together well.

3. Add the butter, then blend it into the dry mix using your hands until it resembled coarse crumbles.

4. Add the eggs, heavy cream and vanilla extract and mix the ingredients together to form a thick dough.

5. Mix in the apple pieces until evenly distributed throughout the dough.

6. Next, turn the dough out onto your floured surface. Then, roll into a ball.

7. Flatten the ball into a 1" thick round disc.

8. Cut the disc into 14 triangles then place then on the prepared sheet tray.

9. Brush the scones with the milk then sprinkle with the white granulated sugar.

10. Bake in the preheated oven for 15 minutes or until the edges are golden brown.

11. Remove the tray from the oven. Then, move the scones to a cooling rack.

12. Enjoy warm!

Lemon Rosemary Scones

These scones have an interesting taste that is unique while also amazingly delicious. Everyone will be asking you for this recipe after just one bite!

Active Time: 15 minutes

Cook Time: 15 minutes

Yield: 10 servings

Ingredients:

- ¼ cup brown sugar
- 2 ¼ cups flour
- 1/8 tsp kosher salt
- 1 ½ tsp chopped rosemary
- 1 tsp lemon zest
- 1 Tbsp baking powder
- 8 Tbsp butter, room temperature
- 2 large eggs
- ½ cup heavy cream
- ½ tsp lemon extract
- 2 Tbsp white granulated sugar
- 2 Tbsp milk

Directions:

1. First, preheat an oven to 350 degrees F and prepared a sheet tray by lining it with a piece of parchment paper.

2. Second, in a large bowl, combine the flour, salt, rosemary, lemon zest, brown sugar and baking powder. Stir to mix together well.

3. Add the butter, then blend it into the dry mix using your hands until it resembled coarse crumbles.

4. Add the eggs, heavy cream and vanilla extract and mix the ingredients together to form a thick dough.

5. Next, turn the dough out onto your floured surface. Then, roll into a ball.

6. Flatten the ball into a 1" thick round disc.

7. Cut the disc into 10 triangles then place then on the prepared sheet tray.

8. Brush the scones with the milk then sprinkle with the white granulated sugar.

9. Bake in the preheated oven for 15 minutes or until the edges are golden brown.

10. Remove the tray from the oven. Then, move the scones to a cooling rack.

11. Enjoy warm!

Citrus Explosion Scones

It is no surprise that citrus goes great in scones. This recipe is packed with citrus tastes that you will go crazy for! These scones are ideal for summer, spring, winter or fall- they are just good any day!

Active Time: 15 minutes

Cook Time: 15 minutes

Yield: 10 servings

Ingredients:

- ¼ cup brown sugar
- 2 ¼ cups flour
- 1/8 tsp kosher salt
- 1 tsp lemon zest
- 1 tsp orange zest
- 1 Tbsp baking powder
- 8 Tbsp butter, room temperature
- 2 large eggs
- ¼ cup heavy cream
- 2 Tbsp fresh lime juice
- 2 Tbsp fresh lemon juice
- 2 Tbsp white granulated sugar
- 2 Tbsp milk

Directions:

1. First, preheat an oven to 350 degrees F and prepared a sheet tray by lining it with a piece of parchment paper.

2. Second, in a large bowl, combine the flour, salt, lemon zest, orange zest, brown sugar and baking powder. Stir to mix together well.

3. Add the butter, then blend it into the dry mix using your hands until it resembled coarse crumbles.

4. Add the eggs, heavy cream, lemon juice and lime juice and mix the ingredients together to form a thick dough.

5. Next, turn the dough out onto your floured surface. Then, roll into a ball.

6. Flatten the ball into a 1" thick round disc.

7. Cut the disc into 10 triangles then place then on the prepared sheet tray.

8. Brush the scones with the milk then sprinkle with the white granulated sugar.

9. Bake in the preheated oven for 15 minutes or until the edges are golden brown.

10. Remove the tray from the oven. Then, move the scones to a cooling rack.

11. Enjoy warm!

Chocolate Scones

Sometimes you need a little bit of chocolate to start your morning off on the right foot. These chocolate scones are decadent and simply amazing- you will want them for breakfast every morning!

Active Time: 15 minutes

Cook Time: 15 minutes

Yield: 10 servings

Ingredients:

- ¼ cup brown sugar
- 1 ¾ cups flour
- 1/8 tsp kosher salt
- ½ cup unsweetened cocoa powder
- 1 Tbsp baking powder
- 8 Tbsp butter, room temperature
- 2 large eggs
- ½ cup heavy cream
- ¾ tsp vanilla extract
- 2 Tbsp white granulated sugar
- 2 Tbsp milk

Directions:

1. First, preheat an oven to 350 degrees F and prepared a sheet tray by lining it with a piece of parchment paper.

2. Second, in a large bowl, combine the flour, salt, cocoa powder, brown sugar and baking powder. Stir to mix together well.

3. Add the butter, then blend it into the dry mix using your hands until it resembled coarse crumbles.

4. Add the eggs, heavy cream and vanilla extract and mix the ingredients together to form a thick dough.

5. Next, turn the dough out onto your floured surface. Then, roll into a ball.

6. Flatten the ball into a 1" thick round disc.

7. Cut the disc into 10 triangles then place then on the prepared sheet tray.

8. Brush the scones with the milk then sprinkle with the white granulated sugar.

9. Bake in the preheated oven for 15 minutes or until the edges are golden brown.

10. Remove the tray from the oven. Then, move the scones to a cooling rack.

11. Enjoy warm!

Double Chocolate Scones

We aren't sure whether these scones should be considered a breakfast or a dessert but we are happy to eat them anytime! They are certainly the perfect amount of sweetness and chocolatey goodness to make your mouth water.

Active Time: 15 minutes

Cook Time: 15 minutes

Yield: 12 servings

Ingredients:

- ¼ cup brown sugar
- 1 ¾ cups flour
- 1/8 tsp kosher salt
- ½ cup unsweetened cocoa powder
- 1 Tbsp baking powder
- 8 Tbsp butter, room temperature
- 2 large eggs
- ½ cup heavy cream
- ¾ tsp vanilla extract
- 1 cup chocolate chips
- 2 Tbsp white granulated sugar
- 2 Tbsp milk

Directions:

1. First, preheat an oven to 350 degrees F and prepared a sheet tray by lining it with a piece of parchment paper.

2. Second, in a large bowl, combine the flour, salt, cocoa powder, brown sugar and baking powder. Stir to mix together well.

3. Add the butter, then blend it into the dry mix using your hands until it resembled coarse crumbles.

4. Stir in the chocolate chips.

5. Add the eggs, heavy cream and vanilla extract and mix the ingredients together to form a thick dough.

6. Next, turn the dough out onto your floured surface. Then, roll into a ball.

7. Flatten the ball into a 1" thick round disc.

8. Cut the disc into 12 triangles then place then on the prepared sheet tray.

9. Brush the scones with the milk then sprinkle with the white granulated sugar.

10. Bake in the preheated oven for 15 minutes or until the edges are golden brown.

11. Remove the tray from the oven. Then, move the scones to a cooling rack.

12. Enjoy warm!

Pumpkin Chocolate Chip Scones

Pumpkin and chocolate chips are a match made in heaven. The warm, melty chocolate chips complement the pumpkin spice taste perfectly. It is a flavor combination that is sure to be one of your favorites.

Active Time: 15 minutes

Cook Time: 15 minutes

Yield: 12 servings

Ingredients:

- 2 ¼ cups flour
- 1/8 tsp kosher salt
- 1 ½ tsp pumpkin spice
- 1 Tbsp baking powder
- ¼ cup brown sugar
- 6 Tbsp butter, room temperature
- ½ cup pumpkin puree
- 1 large egg
- ½ cup heavy cream
- ¾ tsp vanilla extract
- 1 cup chocolate chips
- 2 Tbsp white granulated sugar
- 2 Tbsp milk

Directions:

1. First, preheat an oven to 350 degrees F and prepared a sheet tray by lining it with a piece of parchment paper.

2. Second, in a large bowl, combine the flour, salt, pumpkin spice, brown sugar and baking powder. Stir to mix together well.

3. Add the butter, then blend it into the dry mix using your hands until it resembled coarse crumbles.

4. Stir in the chocolate chips.

5. Add the egg, pumpkin puree, heavy cream and vanilla extract and mix the ingredients together to form a thick dough.

6. Next, turn the dough out onto your floured surface. Then, roll into a ball.

7. Flatten the ball into a 1" thick round disc.

8. Cut the disc into 10 triangles then place then on the prepared sheet tray.

9. Brush the scones with the milk then sprinkle with the white granulated sugar.

10. Bake in the preheated oven for 15 minutes or until the edges are golden brown.

11. Remove the tray from the oven. Then, move the scones to a cooling rack.

12. Enjoy warm!

Oatmeal Lavender Scones

These scones make for the perfect addition to your brunch table. The subtle lavender taste will have everyone asking how you made such these delicious and unique scones! Pair perfectly with tea.

Active Time: 15 minutes

Cook Time: 15 minutes

Yield: 10 servings

Ingredients:

- 1 ¼ cups flour
- 1 cup rolled oats
- 1/8 tsp kosher salt
- 1 tsp ground cinnamon
- 1 tsp lemon zest
- 1 Tbsp baking powder
- ¼ cup brown sugar
- 8 Tbsp butter, room temperature
- 2 large eggs
- ¾ cup heavy cream
- 3 Tbsp dried lavender
- ¾ tsp vanilla extract
- 2 Tbsp white granulated sugar
- 2 Tbsp milk

Directions:

1. First, preheat an oven to 350 degrees F and prepared a sheet tray by lining it with a piece of parchment paper.

2. Place the lavender and heavy cream in a small sauce pan. Bring to a boil, then remove from the heat. Set aside to steep for 10 minutes. Strain the lavender and discard, keeping just the infused heavy cream.

3. In a large bowl, combine the cinnamon, rolled oats, flour, lemon zest, salt, brown sugar and baking powder. Stir to mix together well.

4. Add the butter, then blend it into the dry mix using your hands until it resembled coarse crumbles.

5. Add the eggs, lavender heavy cream and vanilla extract and mix the ingredients together to form a thick dough.

6. Next, turn the dough out onto your floured surface. Then, roll into a ball. Flatten the ball into a 1" thick round disc.

7. Cut the disc into 10 triangles then place then on the prepared sheet tray.

8. Brush the scones with the milk then sprinkle with the white granulated sugar.

9. Bake in the preheated oven for 15 minutes or until the edges are golden brown.

10. Remove the tray from the oven. Then, move the scones to a cooling rack. Enjoy warm!

Honey Scones

A simple, sweet scone that highlights the great taste of honey. Use good, high quality honey for the best results- see if there is local honey available near you and drizzle some extra over a warm scone before you enjoy!

Active Time: 15 minutes

Cook Time: 15 minutes

Yield: 10 servings

Ingredients:

- 2 ½ cups flour
- 1/8 tsp kosher salt
- ¼ cup honey
- 1 Tbsp baking powder
- 8 Tbsp butter, room temperature
- 2 large eggs
- ½ cup heavy cream
- ¾ tsp vanilla extract
- 2 Tbsp white granulated sugar
- 2 Tbsp milk

Directions:

1. First, preheat an oven to 350 degrees F and prepared a sheet tray by lining it with a piece of parchment paper.

2. Second, in a large bowl, combine the flour, salt, and baking powder. Stir to mix together well.

3. Add the butter, then blend it into the dry mix using your hands until it resembled coarse crumbles.

4. Add the eggs, heavy cream, honey and vanilla extract and mix the ingredients together to form a thick dough.

5. Next, turn the dough out onto your floured surface. Then, roll into a ball.

6. Flatten the ball into a 1" thick round disc.

7. Cut the disc into 10 triangles then place then on the prepared sheet tray.

8. Brush the scones with the milk then sprinkle with the white granulated sugar.

9. Bake in the preheated oven for 15 minutes or until the edges are golden brown.

10. Remove the tray from the oven. Then, move the scones to a cooling rack.

11. Enjoy warm!

Orange Brie Scones

The great taste of brie cheese makes these scones a total hit. They are sweet yet salty, brightly flavored yet savory. It is a great way to enjoy a scone in a whole new way!

Active Time: 15 minutes

Cook Time: 15 minutes

Yield: 10 servings

Ingredients:

- 2 ¼ cups flour
- 1/8 tsp kosher salt
- 1 tsp orange zest
- 1 Tbsp baking powder
- ¼ cup brown sugar
- 4 Tbsp butter, room temperature
- 4 ounces creamy brie
- 2 large eggs
- ½ cup heavy cream
- ¾ tsp vanilla extract
- 2 Tbsp white granulated sugar
- 2 Tbsp milk

Directions:

1. First, preheat an oven to 350 degrees F and prepared a sheet tray by lining it with a piece of parchment paper.

2. Second, in a large bowl, combine the flour, salt, orange zest, brown sugar and baking powder. Stir to mix together well.

3. Add the butter and creamy brie and blend it into the dry mix using your hands until it resembled coarse crumbles.

4. Add the eggs, heavy cream and vanilla extract and mix the ingredients together to form a thick dough.

5. Next, turn the dough out onto your floured surface. Then, roll into a ball.

6. Flatten the ball into a 1" thick round disc.

7. Cut the disc into 10 triangles then place then on the prepared sheet tray.

8. Brush the scones with the milk then sprinkle with the white granulated sugar.

9. Bake in the preheated oven for 15 minutes or until the edges are golden brown.

10. Remove the tray from the oven. Then, move the scones to a cooling rack.

11. Enjoy warm!

Orange Dark Chocolate Scones

Fresh orange zest and dark chocolate pair to make a scone fit for any breakfast table. Use dark chocolate or semi-sweet chocolate chips to ensure that the scones aren't too sweet.

Active Time: 15 minutes

Cook Time: 15 minutes

Yield: 12 servings

Ingredients:

- ¼ cup brown sugar
- 2 ¼ cups flour
- 1/8 tsp kosher salt
- 1 Tbsp baking powder
- 1 tsp orange zest
- 8 Tbsp butter, room temperature
- 2 large eggs
- ¼ cup orange juice
- ¼ cup sour cream
- ¾ tsp vanilla extract
- 1 cup dark chocolate chips
- 2 Tbsp white granulated sugar
- 2 Tbsp milk

Directions:

1. First, preheat an oven to 350 degrees F and prepared a sheet tray by lining it with a piece of parchment paper.

2. Second, in a large bowl, combine the flour, salt, orange zest, brown sugar and baking powder. Stir to mix together well.

3. Add the butter, then blend it into the dry mix using your hands until it resembled coarse crumbles.

4. Stir in the chocolate chips

5. Add the eggs, sour cream, orange juice and vanilla extract and mix the ingredients together to form a thick dough.

6. Next, turn the dough out onto your floured surface. Then, roll into a ball.

7. Flatten the ball into a 1" thick round disc.

8. Cut the disc into 12 triangles then place then on the prepared sheet tray.

9. Brush the scones with the milk then sprinkle with the white granulated sugar.

10. Bake in the preheated oven for 15 minutes or until the edges are golden brown.

11. Remove the tray from the oven. Then, move the scones to a cooling rack.

12. Enjoy warm!

Author's Afterthoughts

Thank you for making the decision to invest in one of my cookbooks! I cherish all my readers and hope you find joy in preparing these meals as I have.

There are so many books available and I am truly grateful that you decided to buy this one and follow it from beginning to end.

I love hearing from my readers on what they thought of this book and any value they received from reading it. As a personal favor, I would appreciate any feedback you can give in the form of a review on Amazon and please be honest! This kind of support will help others make an informed choice on and will help me tremendously in producing the best quality books possible.

My most heartfelt thanks,

Nancy Silverman

If you're interested in more of my books, be sure to follow my author page on Amazon (can be found on the link Bellow) or scan the QR-Code.

https://www.amazon.com/author/nancy-silverman

Made in the USA
Las Vegas, NV
15 November 2023

80899282R10057